# DECEPTIVE THREADS

## DAVID JOSEPH AND KAREN BERGER

Currency Press,
Sydney

LA MAMA

CURRENT THEATRE SERIES

First published in 2018
by Currency Press Pty Ltd,
PO Box 2287, Strawberry Hills, NSW, 2012, Australia
enquiries@currency.com.au
www.currency.com.au

in association with La Mama Theatre, Melbourne

Typeset by Dean Nottle for Currency Press.
Cover image by Ponch Hawkes.
Cover design by Emma Rose Smith for Currency Press.
Cover shows David Joseph.
La Mama Schools Publication Coordinator: Maureen Hartley.

Currency Press acknowledges the Traditional Owners of the Country on which
we live and work. We pay our respects to all Aboriginal and Torres Strait
Islander Elders, past and present.

NATIONAL
LIBRARY
OF AUSTRALIA

A catalogue record for this
book is available from the
National Library of Australia

# Contents

## ACKNOWLEDGEMENTS

Bowerbird Theatre would like to extend their deep gratitude to Peter Joseph for his financial support; to Claire Grady and Emma Rose Smith from Currency Press for their editorial support; and to Liz Jones, Maureen Hartley, Caitlin Dullard and all the wonderful staff at La Mama Theatre.

*Deceptive Threads* was first produced by Bowerbird Theatre at Metanoia Theatre, Brunswick, August 2015, with the following participants:

PERFORMER   David Joseph

Devisors, David Joseph and Karen Berger
Director, Karen Berger
Set Designer, David Joseph
Sound Designers, David Joseph and Karen Berger
Lighting Designer, Bronwyn Pringle
        (adapted for La Mama by Gina Gascoigne)
Projection Designers, Zoe Scoglio, David Joseph and Karen Berger
Projection Producer, Zoe Scoglio
Costume Designer, Emily Barrie

*Deceptive Threads* was also produced by Bowerbird Theatre at fortyfivedownstairs, Melbourne, in November 2016, with the same cast and crew, plus the addition of projections by Hisham Tawfiqi.

## CHARACTERS

DAVID, a storyteller

FATE, a crone and weaver of destiny

DETECTIVE

LEBANESE STORYTELLER

ELIAS, David's paternal grandfather

FRED, David's maternal grandfather

POLITICIANS, various from Australian history

All characters are played by a single performer.

This play went to press before the end of rehearsals and may differ from the play as performed.

*The stage is roughly split into two sides.*

*On one side hung four muslin sacks, ranging in size from about 600-centimetre diameter to the size of a fist.*

*Below them sits a vintage overlocker with three large spools.*

*Threads from these spools lead up to entwine with threads from the muslin sacks.*

*Threads and muslin both hang over to the other side of the stage which has two filing cabinets, one with a 1950s typewriter sitting on it.*

*Above this hangs a vintage lampshade.*

*A muslin scrim hangs across the middle upstage area.*

*Above the scrim is a one-metre-wide stretch of empty, white wall, used for projections—the surtitle area.*


SCENE ONE

FATE SEWS AT HER OVERLOCKER

*Muslin from the scrim connects to the overlocker table.*

*Projection (onto the muslin sacks): Water ripples.*

*Music: 'The World's Oldest Melody'—a Hurrian hymn, Syria, c1400 BC.*

*An old crone,* FATE, *enters with a candle and moves to the overlocker.*

FATE: [*addressing the audience and the threads*] *You* that are born of mortal womb are slaves by necessity to me, Fate the sewer. And you shall suffer such things as destiny wove into the strands of your birth that day you were born to your mother and entered this world.

 *She points to three spools on the overlocker.*

The things that were, the things that are and those things that are yet to be. [*To herself*] Get a wiggle on, haven't got all bloody day.

[*Sitting at the overlocker*] You must look to meet whatever the stern sewer twists into the triple threads as they whirl on with the rushing of your destiny.

*She sews with the overlocker.*

[*Picking up a tangle of threads*] History, fiction—interwoven and retold …

*Pointing to threads hanging across the stage:*

… and cosmic time, well, that mediates your mortal rhythms and ties you to those that have come before and those that are yet to be.

*She sews with the overlocker.*

All things must run on in their appointed time, and your first day … well, that fixed your last. Roughly I tear the threads of flourishing life.

*She breaks the thread.*

*Sound: A deep boom.*

FATE *exits with the candle.*

*Projections (onto the muslin sacks, hanging threads, muslin scrim and surtitle area): A close-up of the overlocker mechanism, dancing threads morphing into DNA and, finally, thread magically writing the words 'Looking behind me I see the threads of my ancestors' lives unwinding'.*


*SCENE TWO*

*UNTANGLING DNA*

*A hand appears from a filing cabinet drawer and types on the typewriter.*

*Projection: The typewriter typing 'DNA? Research = mesearch'.*

*The drawer closes.*

*It opens again and the hand throws out DNA letters tied with thread: T, A, C, C, A, G, et cetera.*

*The shadow of a head appears behind the scrim, searching with a torch—an American 1950s* SPY, *in trench coat and hat.*

*He enters through the scrim and discovers the DNA letters.*

*As he picks them up, their shadow appears on the scrim.*

SPY: [*to himself*] T, A, G, tag … C, G, G … It's some kind of code … A, C, C, G, T, A, What the hell is this? T, A, A, C, G, X … Y, X, Y—I got it! It's the code for DNA. Yeah, I remember this malarky from senior high—X and Y, they're the chromosomes. Y, Y, Y … The Y chromosome, that's the one that gets passed unchanged throughout time from father to son to his son, on and on, unbroken …

> *He continues to pull the threads out of the filing cabinet to reveal a muslin scarf with Arabic calligraphy.*
>
> *He lights it with the torch.*

What the heck is this?

> *He finds and reads a tag on the end of the scarf.*

'Ancient Lebanese proverb: "A man can no more forget his father and grandfather than a river can forget its source".'

> *He drops the scarf.*

Baloney! The guy didn't even know his grandfather. His father didn't even know him—he died when he was a baby. How can you forget someone you never even knew?

> *He slams the filing cabinet drawer closed and lights his face from below.*

I feel like I'm being watched.

*He turns the torch to the audience.*

You're watching me.

*As he turns off the torch, the house lights come up.*

DAVID: Well, of course you're watching me— [*Chattily*] I'm an actor, you're the audience—you're here to watch me tell a story, and I'm here to play the roles, to change identities. Hi, I'm Dave …

*During the following* DAVID *takes off the spy hat and coat and places them in one of the filing cabinet drawers.*

So, stories. Here's a real-life story: The strangest thing happened to me—I got caught up in an ancient tradition without being conscious of it. My grandfather, the one I never knew, his name was Elias and his nickname was Eli. Now, I had no idea about that when I named my own son Eli—that's a strange enough coincidence in itself—but then I found out that it's a Lebanese family tradition to name your firstborn son after your grandfather.

*He picks up the DNA letters and places them beside the filing cabinet.*

Maybe the threads connecting me to the past are not as fragile as I think …

*Arabic music fades up.* DAVID *goes behind the scrim.*

*Projection: A family photo with Elias.*

DAVID *stands behind the photo of Elias' face with the torch lighting his face—their two faces combine.*

*SCENE THREE*

*LEBANESE STORYTELLER SPINS THE STORY OF KFARSGHAB*

*Projection (onto the scrim): An image of spinning Arabic calligraphy.*

*A Lebanese* STORYTELLER *enters, with moustache, waistcoat, fez and darbukka, dancing to Persian music.*

*The image crossfades to a photo of an ancient cedar grove on Mount Lebanon.*

STORYTELLER: [*to the audience, as if they're* DAVID] Kiffek, Habibi! Oldest son of the youngest son of the son of the mountain, let me tell you the story of your ancestors. Let me tell you in the tradition of the great Lebanese storytellers.

Daoud, David, your ancestors' village is nestled high in the mountains, near the cedars of God, ancient cedars, holy woods.

> *He opens an old suitcase that is beside the overlocker.*
>
> *He digs in dirt in the suitcase.*
>
> *He finds a Bible in the dirt.*
>
> *Projection: A cedar grove.*

You are digging for roots in a holy forest.

Ahhh! Scribbled in the margins of this ancient Bible is the first written record of your village, Kfarsghab.

> *He drums on the darbukka as he tells the story.*

It records an attack in the year 1283 by the brutal warlords, the Mamelukes. Your ancestors fled to a beautiful and inaccessible grotto …

> *Projection: A cave.*

… where they were besieged for seven long years, suffering vicissitudes and depravations that you could never dream of, the innocent ones born therein never feeling the caress of the sun's warm touch. Meanwhile, the wily Mamelukes, tiring of their vigil, convinced the villagers to descend from their hideaway on the promise of a safe release.

> *He laughs while moving to centre stage, spinning in a tight circle, beating a drum roll as his laughter turns to a scream.*
>
> *This abruptly stops and he breaks out of storytelling mode.*

Do you see? Do you see? I, the Lebanese storyteller, I can confirm all of your preconceptions, misconceptions and stereotypes about the Arab. A mosque in Bendigo … why would you do that? Bendigo has such charming colonial architecture … Now, back to our story …

Oh! How they suffered! The men were swiftly massacred and the women and children taken as hostages and slaves.

*He dances and plays the drum in a funereal style.*

So much suffering … Centuries of bloodshed and violence … Brutal men battling for possession of these mountains, gateway to the splendours of the Holy Lands.

*Projection: The cedar grove.*

For this place was sacred long before our Lord Jesus Christ was born. The holy cedars of Mount Lebanon once sheltered the Sumerian Gilgamesh, hero of the first written story. Noah used these cedars to build his ark, and King Solomon sought them for the construction of his temple. Still they stand, five thousand years old. The Roman Emperor Hadrian, Mameluke caliphs and Maronite patriarchs have all issued decrees protecting the ancient stand. Even her royal highness Queen Victoria deemed them worthy of protection.

But the people of Lebanon have not been so protected.

*He closes the suitcase.*

Many of us have been refugees, fleeing war, turmoil and famine … Daoud! Your grandfather, Elias, was one of them …

*The drumming fades out as the* STORYTELLER *backs out behind the scrim.*

*SCENE FOUR*

*ELIAS' JOURNEY*

*Projection: Bartlett's nineteenth-century print of a Lebanese village, and 'Kfarsghab, Mount Lebanon, 1896' written on the surtitle area.*

*The journey sequence starts as a young* ELIAS *appears, dressed in a cap and jacket.*

*Sound: Village life—chopping wood, villagers bidding Elias farewell et cetera.*

ELIAS *sits on his suitcase as other Bartlett prints are projected and smaller images appear on the suitcase: people working in the fields, camels at an ancient Lebanese ruin.*

*Sound: A busy Arabic port.*

ELIAS *exits.*

*Projection: Images of Port Said, Arabic seamen with huge ropes on the dock, immigrants travelling on a ship's deck. On the suitcase a projection of a postcard of the ship that Elias took to Australia (the* Almeida*), in a stormy sea.*

*Sound: Sister Marie Keyrouz singing 'Alleluia'.*

*Projection: A video of the sea.*

*On the surtitle area, a large rope breaks, a boom is heard and we see* ELIAS *behind the scrim, falling, then somehow floating in this sea.*

*Projection (overlaid): A nineteenth-century map of the Middle East.*

*Sound and projections: An Australian port at the turn of the century—a quay, an immigration arrivals hall.*

*Sound: An official telling people to 'Get a wiggle on!'*

ELIAS *jumps down from behind the scrim and is in Australia.*

*Projections: The Australian bush.*

*Sound: Australian bird sounds.*

ELIAS: [*voice-over*] When I land in Adelaide, they change my name. I am Elias Yusuf Daniel—but the immigration man, he could not understand me, he write down Elias Joseph, so that's who I become.

Oh, it's a beautiful land, this one. When I first come here, a man from my country give me a suitcase [*picking up his suitcase*] full of cotton, coloured ribbons, needles, fancy things. He teach me: 'Hello, missus. This one very nice, two shillings.' I'm walking, selling to the farmers' wives. I stay on the railway line …

*Projection: Workers laying a railway.*

… to not get lost. I save money, I buy a horse and I travel further and further, all the way to Toowoomba …

*Projection: An old photo of Toowoomba.*

… where I married a girl from my village, Em. It was very good to grow vegetables there.

*Projections: A boy working in a market garden. On the suitcase, an image of lemons.*

I bought land and I open a shop to sell all the things I grow. And I would drive to Brisbane markets to buy oranges and lemons to sell to those people in the bush.

When I had children, twelve I had!

*Projection (onto the suitcase and the surtitle area): A family photo.*

My sons would drive for me—they were good mechanics. My daughters—they were dressmakers. The best in town. They were good cooks too—my wife, she taught them to make the labne, just like my mother did, from the real goats' milk, and one of my girls, Nancy, she ran a SP bookie business out of her bedroom window—she loves the horses, that one. You know, they even named a street after me—Joseph Street. Ehhh, it's not even my real surname.

*Projection: The Joseph family shop, zooming in as* ELIAS *enters the scrim through the front door of the shop.*

## SCENE FIVE

## WHITE AUSTRALIA

DAVID *calls from behind the scrim as we see a torchlight searching behind paper sewing patterns attached to the overlocker.*

*The shadow of a hand pushes through the patterns.*

DAVID: Elias … Elias … Eli … Grandfather … Gidi … Gidi?

*Shining the torch on his face:*

I never knew him, but I remember all of this …

*Lights up on labne sacks and the overlocker.*

… the tear-shaped sacks of delicious labne dripping whey into my grandmother's kitchen sink. And these—the table, the overlocker, these patterns—these are from the family business they started in Redfern. They moved there from Toowoomba after my grandfather died.

*Sound: A boom.*

*Projections: An image of Elias' gravestone appears on the patterns, then the scrim and then the surtitle area.*

Alias Joseph? They spelt his name wrong on his gravestone? Alias? Alias Joseph? As if he had something to hide …

*Sound: Typewriter sounds.*

*Projection: Elias' application for naturalisation.*

[*Reading*] 'I, Elias Joseph, Ruthven Street, Toowoomba … I am by birth a Grecian subject … Arrived from Naxos Island. Greece.'

*Projection: An official document requesting to know whether Elias is a 'coloured man'.*

'Hawker, Toowoomba … Whether he is a coloured man?

*Projection: An affidavit used in Elias' application for naturalisation. Important words get projected onto* DAVID*'s back as he walks in front of it, reading aloud some sections:*

[*Reading*] 'Sir … Application for naturalisation … Received from Elias Joseph … I have the honour to inform you that applicant is not a coloured man. When a boy of ten years of age, he went with his parents from Naxos Island to Port Said, where both his parents died. Subsequently coming to Australia, he arrived in Adelaide in 1898. For twelve years he followed the occupation of hawker and was never proceeded against for a breach of the Law. Arrived in Queensland, Toowoomba. In 1910 he married the daughter of an Assyrian storekeeper … Applicant has recently purchased a small farm … In all his business transactions he has proved himself an honest man. He speaks the English language fairly fluently and generally bears a very good character in Toowoomba. The only document he can produce in support of his statement that he was born at Naxos Island, Grecian Archipelago, is his marriage certificate, but all inquiries leave no doubt about his nationality. I have the honour to be, Sir, Your obedient servant …'

*As he finishes reading, he turns to the audience.*

I thought he was Lebanese!—I thought *I* was Lebanese!

*Light comes up suddenly over the filing cabinet.*

DAVID *opens a filing cabinet drawer and pulls out a turn-of-the-century newspaper.*

*Sydney Morning Herald*, 1893. [*Reading aloud*] 'The Lebanese are the most objectionable class to have in any community.'

*He bulldog-clips the newspaper to threads hanging from the ceiling and places it back into the filing cabinet.*

*He pulls out another newspaper.*

The *South Australian Register*, Adelaide 1899. [*Reading*] 'These aliens, the Lebanese, besides breeding disease and hybrid children—neither black nor white nor brindle—live on a lower scale. They are of an inferior race—inferior in morals, inferior in enlightenment, and inferior in standards of living. What have we to gain from them? Considerably less than nothing, for we have all to lose.'

*He bulldog-clips the newspaper to threads and places it back in the filing cabinet.*

*He retrieves another newspaper.*

*Whilst reading the following article,* DAVID *covers his face with the newspaper, becoming an angry, masked newspaper 'monster'.*

The *Argus*, 1900. [*Reading*] 'The town and district of Ballarat are now alive to the serious menace involved in the Lebanese question. What brought the Lebanese here in such numbers and who keeps them here? They came along quickly and unobtrusively like the rabbits at first, but the community has wakened up to find both pests swarming, until the pessimistic prophecy is possible that Ballarat must be given up to the Lebanese and the rabbits. The rabbits may have a share of it, but the Lebanese not a pennyworth more if this journal can by its fearless denunciation prevent them. They are dangerous people, these hawkers, and country people must watch them. It will be a sad day for a White Australia if Lebanese immigration is permitted to continue in this country.'

*This last newspaper is placed in the filing cabinet.*

*From a lower drawer,* DAVID *finds a file containing Government Acts.*

*He stands in front of the filing cabinet and delivers in an official manner:*

1901—Federation—and the First Act of Parliament is the Immigration Restriction Act. ˙The immigration into the Commonwealth of the following persons is prohibited, namely— Any person who when asked to do so by an officer fails to write out at dictation and sign in the presence of the officer a passage of fifty words in length in any European language directed by the officer.'

*In a consoling manner:*

1903—An Act relating to naturalisation. 'The following persons are *not* eligible to apply for a certificate of naturalisation: natives of Asia, Africa, or the Islands of the Pacific, excepting of course, New Zealand.'

*As* DAVID *walks away from the filing cabinet, the file that he's still holding is connected to thread that spools out of the cabinet.*

*The house lights come up as* DAVID *delivers the following speech, initially talking to himself, then getting more involved with the audience.*

White Australia had drawn a line in the sand—and a literal line around the edges of Europe.

*He wraps audience members in the thread.*

Lebanon was just on the wrong side of that line. And so for Elias to secure a future in his new home he had to lie about his birthplace, he had to leap over that line …

*He 'leaps' over the thread.*

… just far enough to be white. Naxos Island was only eight hundred kilometres from Kfarsghab—less than what he'd walked from Adelaide to Toowoomba!

Racism now, racism then … 1903 …

*SCENE SIX*

*ACTS OF PARLIAMENT*

*Sound: Parliamentary hubbub.*

SPEAKER: In support of the Act, Queensland Senator Anderson Dawson would like to make a statement.

DAWSON: There ought, in my opinion, be some differentiation between the coloured alien and the white alien.

*Projection: The word 'Alien' swirls through the space,
becoming the beginnings of a thread.*

SPEAKER: Senator James Styles, you'd like to comment?

STYLES: 'Ere, the coloured races know nothing of our laws and care
less. If they do try to make themselves acquainted with our laws
it is usually for the purpose of evading them. And if the Chinese
have votes, they exercise a privilege …

*Projection: The word 'Privilege' is projected in the same
manner, the thread extends.*

… to which in my opinion they have no right.

*Sound: A typewriter fades in.*

DAVID: 1905 …

SPEAKER: Order, order, gentlemen … The Contract Immigrants
Act. This Act amends and supersedes section 3, paragraph g and
section 11…

*Projection: '3 [g] 11' swirls through the space.*

… of the Immigration Restriction Act of 1901. Prime Minister
Deakin …

DEAKIN: Those whom it was designed to exclude are still prohibited.

SPEAKER: The Member for Echuca, James McColl …

MCCOLL: The policy of a White Australia does not mean that we
should keep Australia for Australians. There are fine …

*Projection: 'Fine'.*

… types of white men in other countries.

DAVID: 1912 …

SPEAKER: The Minister for External Affairs …

MINISTER: I am concerned about considerable leakage …

*Projection: 'Leakage'.*

… under the Immigration Restriction Act, due to a very great
extent to Asian stowaways coming in by the boats.

DAVID: 1939 … Thomas Hugh …

HUGH: [*caught typing on the typewriter*] I wrote to my superior in the Department of the Interior—in a letter marked personal—'Polish Jews are slinking, rat-faced men under five feet high. They are the poorest specimens …

> *Projection: 'Specimens'.*

… outside blackfellows that I have seen.'

SPEAKER: From the Prime Minister's Department …

OFFICIAL: When large numbers arrive by boat the press immediately gives prominence to the fact and strong representations for curtailment of issue of permits are sought.

> *Sound: The typewriter sound distorts and starts to sound like gunshots. It grows louder and starts to drown out the voice of the* SPEAKER.

> *The projected words have all morphed into thread that is being sewn through the scrim by a large needle.*

SPEAKER: Can I draw your attention, members, to the Migration Legislation Amendment Act of 1989, which allows officers to arrest and detain anyone suspected of being an illegal entrant.

Further to that, the Migration Amendment Act of 1992, whereby mandatory detention is envisaged as a temporary and exceptional measure. In the same year, the Reform Act removed the 273-day detention limit. And, in an acknowledgement of the high costs of mandatory detention, the Act introduces detention debts whereby an unlawful non-citizen is liable for the costs of his or her immigration detention.

Excision from Migration Zone [Consequential Provisions] Bill 2001 gives effect to a policy of offshore processing known as the 'Pacific Solution'.

And most recently the Government attempted to introduce legislation to permanently prevent any irregular maritime arrivals from making a valid application for an Australian visa.

*Note: At time of performance, this section can be amended to include the latest news on asylum seeker issues in Australia.*

*The thread continues to sew as a large face fades up on the scrim—we realise that the thread has been sewing an asylum seeker's lips together.*

*Projection: An Australian map showing the excision zone.*

SCENE SEVEN

THREADS OF DNA

*Projection: A DNA map animation showing* DAVID*'s actual DNA results.*

DAVID: Like many of us, I'm questioning my identity—the personal and the political. What is an Australian? So I got my DNA tested.

*He turns and looks at the test results projected on the scrim.*

Italian/Greek: forty percent! What? I don't have any Italian or Greek heritage. … Maybe Elias *was* born on Naxos Island? No, I know he was born in the village on Mount Lebanon! [*Turning to look at the DNA map*] Or is this more about the older history of the Mediterranean, the Greek and Roman Empires?

Ireland: eighteen percent—that'll be all the Nearys in County Clare from Mum's side of the family—the alcoholic priest who lives with his alcoholic mother …

Great Britain: eight percent—that's the second fleeter, who shot dead the escaped Jamaican convict, turned bushranger, Black Caesar … but that's a whole other show.

Middle East: eleven percent; Caucasus: eight percent.

Trace regions.

*Projection: A computer screen cursor appears and* DAVID *clicks on 'trace regions'. The following appears:*

European Jewish: three percent. [*In a Jewish accent*] Who'd a thought? Go figure!

Scandinavia: two percent. Now, that is very interesting because Mum's dad, Fred Ommundson, used to go on about how we were related to the famous Norwegian Arctic explorer, Roald Amundsen. In my mind I'm practically a Viking—well, a Lebanese Viking! Hmmm, there's a big difference between family mythology and scientific reality—between history and fiction.

In fact, there is an old Norwegian saying ...

*He opens the filing cabinet drawer and puts on a policeman's jacket and cap.*

[*In a Norwegian accent*] The coat of truth is often lined with lies. And I think Fred might have worn that coat from time to time.

*He does up the jacket.*

He could definitely spin a good yarn.

## SCENE EIGHT

## A COP'S TALES

FRED: [*a cop*] Yeah, life was tough when I was a tacker. Dad was crippled with arthritis, he wasn't earning tuppence. I had to leave school at fourteen, got a job as an apprentice, never made it to 'you-an-I-verse-city'.

And then, in '37 I think it was, the New South Wales police were running a special recruitment drive—they wanted blokes to go down and stop that damned Victorian polio epidemic from entering New South.

They gave me a uniform and a baton and posted me to Barooga, on the Murray—lovely spot—do you know it? Anyway, I had to stand on that single-lane bridge and stop the cars crossing the border. I'd tell the driver to wind his window down and I'd stick my noggin in, have a bit of a gander, and if anyone looked a bit crook, I made them turn around and go straight back where they came from. I don't know how many healthy people I sent back. I had no medical training. How would I know who had polio and who didn't? I was ordered to use my discretion. What a bloody joke!

Anyway, I liked wearing a uniform—I noticed I got a few extra looks from the lady folk—so when I got back to Sydney I applied for a permanent position in the force. Well, bugger me, I got in and for a bit of a lark I joined the police choir. Well, in the choir, we sang straight stuff, but there were four of us that weren't too bad, and we jazzed it up to have a bit of a laugh. We sang in pubs and at fundraisers et cetera. So then in 1942, one of the fellas entered us in the 2UW amateur hour. We were all on duty that night. We pulled up in our police cars, sirens blaring, leapt out, all in uniform—ran in, sang 'Kentucky Babe' and sped off again. Well, strike me pink, we won! And the next day the police commissioner called us into his office and he bawled us out for taking time off—then he shook our hands and said we were the best damned ambassadors the force had ever had!

Well, our fame continued to spread, and after a couple of years we got offered top billing at Melbourne's Tivoli theatre. One hundred quid a week was more money than we could imagine. The force wouldn't give us leave, so we quit. We called ourselves 'The Four Guardsmen', but Mo, the cheeky bugger, used to call us 'The Four Garbage-men'. He was a card-and-a-half, that bloke.

FRED *exits behind the scrim.*


*SCENE NINE*

*THE TIV*

*The voice-over of an* MC *is heard with:*
*Sound: 1950s showtime music and:*

*Projections: A slide show of Tivoli history.*

MC: [*voice-over*] Ladies and gentlemen, the Tivoli theatre, affectionately known to all who love entertainment as the Tiv, established in 1893 at the old Opera House in Sydney. Bubbling over with action, comedy, colour and charm. Featuring the greatest variety bill ever presented and a brilliant constellation of overseas stars—Harry Houdini, Gracie Fields, Winnie Atwell, and Sir Laurence Olivier. This gay and sparkling revue is your rendezvous with rhythm—where beautiful showgirls parade and dance. Home to Australia's favourite comic, Roy Rene, better known to us all as Mo. Now fifty years on and still going strong. Visiting all the important Australian metropoli—Melbourne, Sydney, Brisbane and Toowoomba.

And introducing our newest act, sure to win a place in the hearts of all music lovers, the kings of comic harmony—The Four Guardsmen. (Black and White cigarettes are always used in Tivoli productions—the artists prefer them!)

*Projections: A Four Guardsmen slide show with:*

*Sound: A recording of The Four Guardsmen singing 'Sweet Kentucky Babe', 'Powder Your Face with Sunshine' and 'The Same Ol' Shillelagh'.*

*SCENE TEN*

*FRED'S SECRET REVEALED*

*Projection: The last image of The Four Guardsmen is of their faces poking through sheet music.*

DAVID *positions himself behind the scrim, behind the image of Fred's face.*

*As the music fades,* DAVID *pokes his head through the muslin.*

FRED: In my experience, musicians are the scum of the earth.

DAVID: [*entering through the scrim*] I'll never forget when Fred said that to me. It was after Mum and Dad had got divorced, and Fred thought some discipline would be good for his eldest grandson. He suggested Duntroon military academy. So I applied for a scholarship, and I got it, but I was too young so I repeated Year Eleven. Fate, huh? I met a whole new bunch of guys. They were the arty, muso, theatre gang, and I'd finally found my tribe. I'd always loved tapping along to songs when I was a kid, but now all of a sudden I was playing drum kit in this teenage psychedelic rock band called Reg Mushroom and we were playing all the cool parties and chicks were throwing themselves at me and I'd finally found my purpose in life!

So … it was Christmas lunch, 1980, and I very proudly announced to the assembled family that I wasn't going to go to Duntroon military academy—I was going to go to art school, I was going to become a muso. And that's when Fred said to me, 'In my experience musicians are the scum of the earth'.

*A phone rings.*

*To answer,* DAVID *opens a filing cabinet drawer.*

[*On the phone*] Hello?

TRISH: [*voice-over*] Oh, hi darling, how are you?

DAVID: [*on the phone*] Oh, Mum! Hi! How are you going?

TRISH: [*voice-over*] I'm fine, I'm really fine. How's everything going?

DAVID: [*on the phone*] Ah, good, but I'm in the middle of a show at the moment …

TRISH: [*voice-over*] Like, you're actually in the middle of a show so I shouldn't be talking?

DAVID: [*on the phone*] No, no, it's okay, what's up?

TRISH: [*voice-over*] Oh, no, no, it's just that I was remembering today some stuff about my dad, and I remember going to this afternoon tea … One of the women there just happened to say, 'So, Fred, are you still working for the Secret Service?'

DAVID: [*on the phone*] What?

TRISH: [*voice-over*] Well, you know, that really just didn't mean anything to me, it went over my head. The next day he probably thought about it, and he probably thought I'd wondered what was going on, so he decided to tell me. I can still see us, sitting in the car, driving along Anzac Parade, and he sort of said, 'Well, you know yesterday when—' and this woman's nickname was Chooky, her real name was Beryl but for some reason she was called Chook and we kids called her Chooky—he said, 'You know when Chooky said something about me working for the Secret Service?', and I must have said, 'Yes'. And he said, 'Well', I think he said, 'Well, yes, it is something like that, what I do, it's very important'. That we were not to discuss it at all. And to be honest, all I remember is thinking, 'Oh, gee, I wish I could go to school and tell everybody—that'd make me important'.

> *As the lights fade,* DAVID *very slowly reaches down into the filing cabinet and during the rest of the conversation dresses in a 1950s spy overcoat and trilby.*

Oh dear, so silly. So that's the first time I really knew. But when I look back now I can remember various things as a very young child.

DAVID: [*on the phone*] Oh, yeah, like what sort of stuff?

TRISH: [*voice-over*] I remember particularly one phone call because it wasn't long after we had the phone put on. And this man rang and asked for Mr Jenkins. Which, you know, I knew nothing about Mr Jenkins, and must have told him, 'No, sorry, you've got the wrong number,' and hung up. But I mentioned it to Mum and she said, 'No, you must always tell me whoever rings. Anybody rings, just get me'. So that was also obviously some kind of connection going on there.

DAVID: [*on the phone*] Yeah, I guess it was his alias.

TRISH: [*voice-over*] And there were periods when he was away for a while. You know, he'd be away for a week or maybe two … and I vaguely remember one particular time when he was pretty nasty when he came back, in fact he seemed to be in a bit of a state when he came home, and very stressed.

DAVID: [*on the phone*] That's really interesting because I remember reading that the CIA sent their agents on torture camps to prepare them in case they were captured. Do you think that ASIO were doing a similar thing?

TRISH: [*voice-over*] Well, I think they would have been. But, you know, you don't, you just don't think about it at the time. Well, when we were small children, you just accept that your father is what he says he is. So that, you know, I've been, I have been trying to think more about if I could find other memories, but that's about it.

## SCENE ELEVEN

## FRED COMES CLEAN

DAVID *slams the filing cabinet door closed.*

*Dressed now as* FRED *the spy, he turns upstage.*

FRED *is side-lit by film noir light.*

*He opens his coat, onto which is projected 1950s ASIO surveillance footage.*

*Sound: Dramatic spy music.*

FRED *closes the coat and tips up the hat.*

FRED: The name's Fred Ommundson, Jenkins is my alias, I work for ASIO, C Branch. I keep unwanted aliens out of Australia, I keep our way of life secure … I keep families apart, I keep fathers away from their children, and I keep wives lonely—what was his name? Yeah, the kids, they wrote letters to the PM, said they wanted their dad back. Moscow—it's a bloody long way away …

> [*Singing*] Maybe I should have kept singing,
> I was so happy back then,
> Life on the road
> With all those Tivoli dancing girls …

[*Talking again*] The lights, the stage, the curtains—I was sent behind the Iron Curtain, you know. Stationed in Rome, trips to Vienna, Yugoslavia, Czechoslovakia—it was during the revolution. Exciting times, you wouldn't be dead for quids, and quids are important. I mean touring with the Tivoli, that was fun, but the money had started to dry up. They started going for those big overseas acts. Now, at the same time, the new head of ASIO, Colonel Spry, was recruiting ex-police officers, so when he called me I jumped at the chance ... It was important work, and I had five hungry kids to feed ...

Frankl, Abe Frankl, that was his name. Poor bastard, didn't see his kids for thirty years ... And then there was the Petrov Affair, what a bloody dog's breakfast that was—'51, peak of the Cold War, I was handler for a Russian-speaking Polish agent sent to watch a Ukrainian doctor, employed by us to befriend Vladimir Petrov. We were never sure whether he was a double agent—the doctor I mean, not Petrov. Petrov? He was just a disgruntled clerk running a sly grog shop out of the Russian embassy. Menzies' Cold War triumph—what a joke! Yeah, well that's enough of that ...

*He raises his finger to his lips.*

FRED *exits into a projection on the scrim of rows of filing cabinets.*

*Sound: A distorted typewriter.*

*Projection: An actual letter from contemporary National Archives.*

DAVID *enters with the letter.*

DAVID: This is the letter I received from the National Archives denying me access to my grandfather's ASIO files. [*Reading from the letter*] 'Reasons for decision—the contents of these files could reasonably be expected to cause resentment and possible retaliation on the part of foreign governments and thus discredit Australia's international reputation.'

## SCENE TWELVE

## BEATING BUREAUCRACY

DAVID *files the letter in the filing cabinet, and pulls out another piece of paper, which he holds up.*

*Projections (onto the paper): Photographs of Fred, then Elias, then David.*

DAVID *pulls open the bottom drawer.*

*Projections (onto the filing cabernet drawer): ASIO surveillance film.*

DAVID *drums a swing jazz rhythm on the sheets of paper.*

*The rhythm builds as he starts to drum on the filing cabinets.*

*Projections build as the drumming builds.*

*These projections are a summary of the story so far—Elias, Fred, ASIO files—but also images that allude to other things—an old padlock, a lemon, a ticking clock stuck on the same time.*

DAVID *climbs onto the filing cabinet.*

*Blackout.*

DAVID *pokes his head out the filing cabinet, looks around and then disappears.*

*Projections start again with the drumming, both building in speed and intensity as the scene climaxes.*

*The projections this time are more overtly directed at Australian racism towards immigrants with images of Pauline Hanson, Peter Dutton, a badge of the Australian Border Force, a 'No Way—You Will Not Make Australia Home' poster, antique White Australia badges.*

*Blackout.*

*SCENE THIRTEEN*

*SHARING LABNE NOW*

*Lights and ancient music fade up slowly.*

DAVID *unties threads of the smallest muslin sack to reveal labne.*

*He prepares the labne with olive oil and salt—the process fitting in with the following text.*

DAVID: When you start to untangle the threads that connect you to the past, and uncover what has been lost, forgotten or secreted away, you see that you have been moulded by those threads, that you are a mixture brought together by those threads of the past into the present which you share with your contemporaries, all of us— children of the past and of this moment, now.

DAVID *shares labne and pita bread with the audience.*

## THE END

# LA MAMA

presents

# DECEPTIVE THREADS

25 April–13 May 2018

Devisors
**David Joseph and Karen Berger**

Director
**Karen Berger**

Set Designer
**David Joseph**

Sound Designers
**David Joseph and Karen Berger**

Lighting Designer
**Bronwyn Pringle**
**adapted for La Mama by Gina Gascoigne**

Projection Designers
**Zoe Scoglio, David Joseph and Karen Berger**

Projection Producer
**Zoe Scoglio**

Additional Visuals
**Hisham Tawfiqi**

Performed by **David Joseph**

bowerbird
THEATRE

A Bowerbird
Theatre
production

# LA MAMA

CEO & Artistic Director
**Liz Jones**

CEO and Manager / Producer
**Caitlin Dullard**

Venue Manager
**Hayley Fox**

Front-of-House Manager
**Amber Hart**

Marketing and Communications
**Sophia Constantine**

Design and Social Media
**Jen Tran**

Office Coordinator
**Elena Larkin**

Learning Producer and School Publications Coordinator
**Maureen Hartley**

Preservation Coordinator
**Fiona Wiseman**

La Mama Musica Curator
**Annabel Warmington**

La Mama Poetica Curator
**Amanda Anastasi**

Script Appraiser
**Graham Downey**

Casting Service
**Zac Kazepis**

Level 1, 205 Faraday Street, Carlton VIC 3053
www.lamama.com.au | info@lamama.com.au
facebook.com/lamama.theatre | twitter.com/lamamatheatre
Office phone 03 9347 6948 | Office Mon–Fri, 10:30am–5:30pm

## FRONT OF HOUSE STAFF

Susan Bamford-Caleo, Carmelina Di Guglielmo, Laurence Strangio,
Dennis Coard, Darren Vizer, Robyn Clancy, Zac Kazepis, Aaron
Bradbrook, Anna Ellis, Alex Woollatt, Annie Thorald, Helen Doig.

## COMMITTEE OF MANAGEMENT

Sue Broadway, David Levin, Caroline Lee, Dur-é Dara,
Richard Watts, Helen Hopkins, Beng Oh, Ben Grant, Liz Jones.

Our sincerest thanks to the many volunteers who generously give
their time in support of La Mama.

La Mama's Committee of Management, staff and its wider
theatrical community acknowledge that our theatre is on traditional
Wurundjeri land.

The La Mama community acknowledges the considerable support
it has received in the past decade from Jeanne Pratt and The Pratt
Foundation.

La Mama is financially assisted by the Australian Government
through the Australia Council – its arts funding and advisory body,
the Victorian Government through Creative Victoria – Department
of Premier and Cabinet, and the City of Melbourne through the Arts
and Culture triennial funding program.

Australian Government

Australia Council
for the Arts

CREATIVE VICTORIA

CITY OF
MELBOURNE

David Joseph in *Deceptive Threads*. Photograph by Ponch Hawkes.

# DEVISOR-PERFORMER'S NOTE

This show was inspired by ancestor worship shrines that I had seen whilst touring through Asia. Ubiquitous and beautiful, they represent a living connection to the past and offer a chance for reflection on the lives that have preceded and shaped these communities.

In 2013 I started the Victorian University Solo Residency and was afforded a year of research and development on a performance piece. I decided to create a theatrical honouring of my ancestors and began the journey of investigation that culminated in *Deceptive Threads*.

On both sides of my family there had always been intriguing stories, half-truths and mysterious secrets surrounding my grandfathers Elias Joseph (a 19th-century Lebanese immigrant) and Fred Ommundson (a singer and spy). In the untangling of the hidden narratives of these two men I discovered a link to our nation's racist past and its connection to our current dilemma over refugees. This immediately struck a chord in me and it became obvious that I had the makings of a show.

As my year at Victoria University came to a close and with my research barely scratching the surface, my supervisor Ben Rogan suggested that I take my study a step further to fully explore the theatrical potential of the material. And so in 2014 I began an MA in Applied Theatre Studies at the University of New England, which offered me the incredible opportunity to delve deeply and systematically into the themes as they unfolded. I also received funding from the Australia Council for a creative development of the work, to fully investigate working the various performance modalities into a cohesive whole.

The show brings to light important global issues of race, place, belonging, identity and undisclosed histories. It also looks at the nexus between the government control of immigration and the 'unwelcome' immigrant. My grandfathers' secret identities embody the notion of a contested, performative space that is reflected in the world of the stage. Familial histories, in particular those that have an element of secrecy surrounding them, can play an important role in expanding our notions of historiography. The disclosure of such secrets can throw light on forgotten characters and events, encouraging a more critical and honest reflection of history.

*Deceptive Threads* won the Khayrallah Art Prize in 2015 for best international artwork expressing the Lebanese diasporic experience (awarded by North Carolina State University) and the Philip Parsons Prize for best practice-as-research project in 2017, awarded by the Australasian Association for Theatre, Drama and Performance Studies.

**David Joseph**
Devisor and performer

# DEVISOR-DIRECTOR'S NOTE

Working on *Deceptive Threads* has been an amazing journey. We visited the National Film and Sound Archives to watch 1950s footage of David's paternal grandfather Fred Ommundson singing in his barbershop quartet, the Four Guardsmen, with American folk legend Burl Ives. We visited the State Library to source rare images of other Tivoli acts (I especially love the photo of a detective investigating the fire that burnt down the Sydney Tivoli, caught from behind dressed in a tutu – see if you can spot it!). We rummaged around the basement of David's maternal family home in Coogee, rescuing from destruction brown paper dress patterns, huge spools of thread and a 1930s overlocker.

Most importantly, we found old photos and documents from the back of drawers that revealed secrets about the family patriarch Elias Joseph that were a surprise to the whole family. The Coogee house was demolished in 2017.

Using Google Maps we found Joseph St in Toowoomba, named after Elias, and tried to discover where his greengrocer shop was. On eBay David bought sheet music published with photos of the Four Guardsmen bursting through the score. I met up with David's mum in Hobart to recreate the phone call where she told David her earliest memories of finding out that her father was a spy – David's step-Dad squashing himself into a cupboard to try and record the best sound quality.

We waited anxiously for ASIO to get back to us with more information about Fred's covert activities and read about Australia's immigration history in Klaus Neumann's comprehensive book *Across the Seas*. I never knew that after Federation, Australia's first act of parliament was the racist Immigration Restriction Act, precursor to the notorious White Australia Policy.

We waited with excitement to read what David's actual DNA makeup is. We invited the Lebanese neighbours to tea to record them pretending to bid farewell to their son leaving for Australia in the 1800s. And David even went into the detail of researching birds living in the Lebanese mountains to create the soundscape – Australian bird sounds were easy!

We delved further into the past, researching stories of cave sieges in ancient Mt Lebanon and finding old lithographs of the beautiful cedars that grow there. Even further back: prayers to Mesopotamian goddesses regarding goat's milk and ancient Greek chants asking for mercy from the Fates. We chose the Arabic darabuka (drum) rhythms that can best be played at the same time as dancing and telling these stories.

Thanks to generous friends, David and I put all this material together at the Edna Walling cottage in Sherbrooke where we were visited by a large flock of satin bowerbirds (they have the most amazing violet-coloured eyes!). Thank you, David, for asking me to join you on this wonderful journey.

**Karen Berger**
Devisor and director

David Joseph in *Deceptive Threads*. Photograph by Steve Willis.

# DESIGN NOTES

## THEMATIC CONCEPT

Threads – a beautiful metaphor for so many things. David grew up around threads – in threads in fact! Bins of sewing offcuts and overlocker ends (smelling of Lebanese sweat!) from his family's rag trade business. He spent hours playing in these threads – an apt symbol for a show about unravelling family secrets, encapsulating both aesthetic and thematic ideas. The vintage overlocker table and sewing machine in the show are from the family business, and the threads that extend from them are woven, literally and figuratively, into the other narratives, histories, genetic lines and lives that extend out from David. All of us are in this same way woven into the fabric of our existence, through family, society and the self. History lives in us, and it is incumbent on each generation to tell the stories that matter from preceding generations. Theatre is arguably the best artform for storytelling, and is a great tool in the quest to disclose history's secrets. Full of metaphor, illusion, meta-narratives and cold hard fact, the very conceit of theatre lends it the possibility of truth, or to paraphrase Picasso, it is 'the lie that reveals the truth'.

## SET DESIGN

All of the set pieces on stage right are from David's paternal side of the family. At the rear of stage right hang muslin sacks of varying sizes, representing bags of labne, a Middle Eastern delicacy of drained yoghurt. In front of these are an antique sewing table and overlocker, part of David's family's rag trade business. Threads from the overlocker extend towards the roof and join with the tops of the muslin bags to form an entwined bunch of threads, which cross the stage and fall again.

Stage left represents David's maternal side of the family. A muslin scrim hangs upstage centre, above which there is another narrow screen, the surtitle area. All of these set pieces also act as screens for projections.

## PROJECTION DESIGN

The projection-mapping design is a complex combination of sourced and original video, still images, archival documents and family photos. They are projected onto all of the set as well as the actor's body and costume, creating a rich visual aesthetic – at times explanatory and text-based and at other times metaphoric and illusory. The melding of sophisticated projection-mapping techniques with accomplished stagecraft allows for a kind of magic realism where the actor can transcend time and space, floating between past and present, memory and illusion.

## SOUND DESIGN

The soundscape is rich and complex, comprising music, sound effects, voices and live percussion. At times the soundscape operates like a movie soundtrack. For example, when David's paternal grandfather Elias travels from Lebanon to Australia. this is told completely through image and sound. The soundscape was comprised of music, voice-overs, recordings of a Lebanese family (recorded in David's kitchen!), and ambient environmental sounds (e.g. Lebanese and Australian birdsong, trees felling, dogs barking, wharf sounds, goats bleating). When revealing David's maternal grandfather's time on the Tivoli circuit, actual recordings of his barbershop quartet accompany a slideshow of their publicity shots.

## LIGHTING DESIGN

The lighting design is simple yet creative, incorporating conventional theatre lights as well as torches, candles, fairy lights and shadow play.

David Joseph in *Deceptive Threads*. Photograph by Ponch Hawkes.

# DAVID JOSEPH
## DEVISOR / PERFORMER

# KAREN BERGER
## DEVISOR / DIRECTOR

**David Joseph** is a professional multi-skilled physical performer with over 30 years experience in the performing arts. He works as an actor, musician, physical performer and teacher and has toured extensively in Australia and internationally. He plays drums for the ARIA winning 26-piece Melbourne Ska Orchestra, as well as being a trained cook and gardener. In 2016 he completed a Masters of Applied Theatre Studies at the University of New England, for which he received the Philip Parsons Prize for best performance-as-research project (ADSA). He is currently studying Landscape Design at Melbourne Polytechnic.

**Karen Berger**'s directing projects include *Barassi: The stage show*, *The Many Walls of Edna Walling*, *The Last Antigone* and *Second City* (all by Tee O'Neill); *The Parricide* (Diane Stubbings), and *The Cosmic Joker* (Alice Springs Festival). In 2016 she was assistant director to Susie Dee on the MTC's production *Peddling*. Musical directing includes *The Penelopiad* (Women's Circus); *Walk on Water* and *Song of Longing* (Anne O'Keeffe); and *Bremen, The Golem of Ruckers Hill* and *The Magic Teapot* (Michael Camilleri). She has an undergraduate degree in music performance and a graduate diploma in Animateuring from the Victorian College of the Arts. She received an award for her MA in Performance Studies from Victoria University.

# BRONWYN PRINGLE
## LIGHTING DESIGNER

**Bronwyn Pringle** is a lighting designer and technician who has worked around Australia with companies such as La Mama, Malthouse, Theatre in Decay, Stuck Pigs Squealing, Here Theatre, Impro Melbourne, Ballarat Arts Academy, Arts Projects Australia and Polyglot Theatre. She has worked on projects from large festivals to small development pieces in venues that include the Sydney Opera House, a London West End nightclub, the Kuala Lumpur Performing Arts Centre, a warehouse in Buenos Aires, the Federation Square air-conditioning ducts and a wool shed in Glencoe, plus many more conventional and non-conventional theatre spaces. Bronwyn's teaching credits include VCA, NMIT, VUT, the Women's Circus and Monash University.

# ZOE SCOGLIO
## PROJECTION DESIGNER

**Zoe Scoglio**'s practice unites performance, video, sound and installation to create inter-disciplinary, site-responsive and participatory pieces. Her work explores how narratives about humanness impact the way we commodify, consume and value the natural world and its resources. Her practice draws upon training in media arts, voice and body-centred practice. Her projects explore possibilities for collective engagement, cere-monial encounters and enlivened installations. She is interested in how video can be sculptural, sound can be physical, and how the body can be a site for enacted geomorphologies.

# HISHAM TAWFIQI
## ADDITIONAL VISUALS

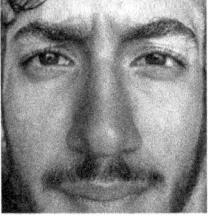

**Hisham Tawfiqi**, born in Bahrain, is an experimental artist who specialises in 3D projection mapping and video animations. His company Vuruz Vision has a mission to open new doors of perception through visual projections.

# STANDING OVATION FOR
# AUSTRALIA'S HOME OF INDEPENDENT THEATRE

In 2018 La Mama will celebrate 51 years of nurturing new Australian theatre.

Built in 1883 for Anthony Reuben Ford, a Carlton printer, the building at 205 Faraday Street had been used as a workshop, a boot and shoe factory, an electrical engineering workshop and a silk underwear factory before becoming a theatre in 1967. La Mama was established by Betty Burstall and modelled on experimental theatre activities at La MaMa E.T.C., New York. Jack Hibberd's play *Three Old Friends* was the first play performed in the tiny space.

Since that time the crowded intimacy of La Mama has provided welcome opportunities to a host of playwrights, actors, directors, technicians, film-makers, poets and comedians, such as David Williamson, Barry Dickins, John Romeril, Tes Lyssiotis, Lloyd Jones, Arthur and Corinne Cantrill, Judith Lucy, Richard Frankland, Julia Zemiro, and Cate Blanchett... the list of those who have been nurtured there is long.

Under the capable care of Liz Jones (Artistic Director since 1976), and her La Mama team, more than 50 productions are now produced annually at La Mama, and at our second performance venue, the refurbished La Mama Courthouse, 349 Drummond Street. An ever-increasing audience is drawn not only from the Carlton and Melbourne University environs, but from far and wide across the country.

'I set La Mama up, as a space for writers and directors to perform in but also it was a space where people came, as audience, to participate in the creative experiment.'

—Betty Burstall, Artistic Director of La Mama 1967–76

'Much will be said of La Mama's role in developing a new generation of Australian writing. However, in considering policies and personalities, one should not forget the nature of the space and its impact in making possible performances that would be lost in a large theatre. It gave performances the intimacy of the cinema close-up with the exciting immediacy of the live theatre and the warmth of the coffee lounge.'

—Daryl Wilkinson, Director

La Mama Theatre—which, on various occasions, has been called headquarters, the source, the shopfront and the birthplace of Australian theatre—was classified by the National Trust in 1999.

'The two-storey brick building is of State cultural significance because it has been occupied by La Mama Theatre... The building is indelibly associated with the performance arts and is a rare manifestation of an experimental theatre in Australia...'

—National Trust Classification Report

'When it comes to grassroots Melbourne theatre, La Mama in Carlton is like the 60GB iPod—small, subtle, but containing a whole lot more than you might expect.'

—John Bailey, Age

La Mama produces work from two venues: 205 Faraday Street, Carlton (opposite top), and at the La Mama Courthouse, 349 Drummond Street, Carlton.

For current La Mama productions and events, see www.lamama.com.au.

www.ingramcontent.com/pod-product-compliance
Lightning Source LLC
Chambersburg PA
CBHW050028090426
42734CB00021B/3465